RESTLESS FOR WORDS:
POEMS

poems by

DeWitt Henry

Finishing Line Press
Georgetown, Kentucky

RESTLESS FOR WORDS:
POEMS

Copyright © 2023 by DeWitt Henry
ISBN 979-8-88838-125-0 First Edition
All rights reserved under International and Pan-American Copyright Conventions. No part of this book may be reproduced in any manner whatsoever without written permission from the publisher, except in the case of brief quotations embodied in critical articles and reviews.

ACKNOWLEDGMENTS

The author is grateful to the editors of the journals in which some of the poems in this book first appeared, sometimes in slightly different versions.

"On Shadows, "On Lust" *Plume*; "On Place," "On Agency," "On Glamor," "On Ghosts," *On the Seawall;* "**On Statues,**" *Woven Tale Press;* "**On Candidates,**" "**On Rank,**" "**On Despair,**" *Ibbetson Street;* "**3 Takes On Spirit,**" "**On Confluence,**" "**On Levity,**" *Muddy River Poetry Review,* "**On Bars,**" *TheNewVerseNews,* "**On Design,**" *Unlikely Stories.* "**On Wonder,**" *Constellations,* "**On Property,** " *American Journal of Poetry;* "**Ordeals,**" "**Mapping,**" *Axon.*

Publisher: Leah Huete de Maines
Editor: Christen Kincaid
Cover Art: *Requiem* by John Friedericy
Author Photo: DeWitt Henry
Cover Design: Elizabeth Maines McCleavy

Order online: www.finishinglinepress.com
also available on amazon.com

Author inquiries and mail orders:
Finishing Line Press
P. O. Box 1626
Georgetown, Kentucky 40324
U. S. A.

Table of Contents

PART ONE

On Shadows 1

On Mapping 3

On Place 6

On Faces 7

On Character 10

On Compensation 13

On Property 15

PART TWO

Doctor 21

On Ghosts 24

On Statues 28

On Rank 32

On Candidates 34

On Agency 35

On Despair 37

On Ordeals 40

PART THREE

On Versions 45

On Confluence 47

On Design 49

On Wonder 52

On Glamor 54

On Lust 58

On Levity 61

On Germans 62

On Modes 63

PART FOUR

On Trees 69

Leaves 72

On Privacy 76

On Distances 80

Lost 83

For my sister, Judith Friedericy

Epigraph:

"*The rest is silence*" (Hamlet)

PART ONE

ON SHADOWS

Me and my shadow
Peter Pan lost his
a shadow of my former self
the Shadow knows
ninety degrees in the shade

like silence to sound,
eddies behind boulders,
eclipses, moon phases
warm-up acts to celebrity.

Sundial's stylus, marking time
Five o'clock shadow

Fencing with his shadow
Scared of her shadow
Groundhog back to sleep

In Science we measured
our shadows according to
the hour and season.
My hand and fingers make a rabbit.
Silhouettes on the shade.
Shapes cast on a backlit screen.
Shades in the underworld.
Overshadowed. Under the shadow.
To shadow is to imitate, to follow.
The P.I. shadows the adulteress.

At 22, a graduate student,
lonely, life- and draft-deferred,
I sat with back to sun, relieved
to spy my head and shoulders
framed by blocks of light.
To have some substance. Self-
defined and fixed upon
a life of thought.

The wicker basket
left outside all winter
leans 0-shaped against a drainpipe,
one side aglow with morning sun
while the other casts its filigree
not only over woven innerness
and rag of snow below, but over
six feet of flat ground
to a wedge-shaped bulkhead,
where it climbs and joins
the solid shadow of the wall,
then lays its crescent handle
(turned to knifepoint)
over one door. Miraculous!

Shadows in her childhood
swept up bedroom walls
as terrors until
"I figured it out one night,"
writes Annie Dillard. Headlights
passing in the street.

We're walking shadows
Poor players, protests the nihilist
Macbeth.

Victims of significance.
Body against soul.
Touch against desire.

Undreamt of transformations,
familiar, yet strange.

ON MAPPING

I like knowing my way without a map.
Like giving directions (more than asking, I admit).
Like knowing short cuts, mastering terrains:
my boyhood home of Wayne PA
(revisited for a 50th high school reunion).
My Watertown neighborhood west of Boston;
Boston itself and the surrounding burbs.
New here as a grad student, I learned my way
by getting lost. Kept a street map in my car.
"No particular place to go," sang Chuck Berry.

"I see (as in a map) the end of all,"
says Queen Elizabeth in Richard III; no palmist,
but could have been, reading fate's trails.

I click on Google Earth, enter my address,
watch the satellite image of North America
zoom to the Northeast, to Boston, to Watertown,
to my street and house. See an aerial photo
from last fall, last bright leaves on trees,
red Ford Focus (since replaced by gray
Honda Fit). At max zoom, everything blurs.

Fun to try my sister's Pasadena address
where I haven't been in years, although
we keep in touch and she's often in mind.
On past visits I learned her streets and town.

Boy Scout woodcraft taught me
to read the stars, the compass,
follow the stream or river,
follow trails and mark them.

After years of using road maps,
I key in the address on my i-phone, choose
shortest route; on screen, a map appears;
a marker follows my progress. The female voice

alerts me to turns or tells me
to continue straight. If I miss
or make a wrong turn, she recalculates.
At destination announces, "You have arrived."
I'll never be lost again, as long as
I'm in the USA and the signal is strong.

The GPS satellite passeth understanding,
like Santa Claus or God, simultaneously,
each instant, listening to every wish,
and tracking every car and route.

No more terra incognita? No trails
to blaze? No ocean depths? We act as if.
Exploring in our bodies, minds, and
outer space. Calculating velocities
and vectors to the moon, then Mars.
Extra-terra incognita. Mapping
surfaces we've never walked.

An age of probes and drones and MRI.
Cartographers of the brain. Here
the regions of love and fear.
Here memory, short or long term.
Here imagination. Circuits like the Interstate.

Overland trails become roads.
Sea roads, ocean charts. Genghis Kahn's
Silk Road. Our Oregon Trail. Our
National Road (now US 40). In crowded skies
flightpaths, skirting storms and traffic.
Earth shrinks. Perspectives, peoples, trade
are woven into states, nations, inter-nations.
And then the internet. Hive mind!

X marks the spot. And what of time?
Identity? The child is father of the man.
We search in different mirrors, he and I,
each with his own desert places.

There, that youth, so full of dreams
and arrogance, he can't conceive
of this autumnal self, except
in scorn and disbelief. Could I comfort
or advise him? Can he sympathize, embrace?
Can we admit and wish each other well?

What else is memory, but mapping the heart?
Like feeling your way into a dark room,
even if you've seen it once in light.

ON PLACE

Backed up at the supermarket checkout, you have forgotten an item; "Hold my place?" you ask the person behind you, so you can go find it. Checked out, then, you roll your cart to your car in its parking place. You head from there to your living place. This may be your home town, or you may be out of place. You may be a tourist, visitor, alien, or drifter, passing through; perhaps you're couch surfing at a friend's. As for me, I stop at my favorite watering place, though I don't look to socialize (no "Your place or mine?"). To regulars, I am commonplace. I may or may not be in a good place. Home is where, when you go there, they have to take you in. When we say place, we often mean space. A space for this life. Elbow room. A room of one's own. Sometimes a transit space. Between habitats, natural or alien. Littoral zone. Comfort zone. Water or land? Gills or lungs? Fish or fowl? Amphibian? What is a leopard doing at this altitude? Hers, His, & Ours. Win, place, or show. Dream place. Peaceable kingdom. Spaces we share. Meeting place. Marketplace. New heavens, new earth. Over the rainbow, where witches fly. Jumping off place. Shelter in place. Placeless places. Places between places. Drifter, vagrant. Trespasser. Private or shared? Rooted, or up-? I have traveled a great deal in Concord. Immigrant. Asylum seeker. Refugee. Give me your tired, your poor. Adopted place. Oriented, disoriented; estranged, familiar. True North. Lost in translation. You are here, or there. Fitting in. Sticking out. Globe trekker. Snowbird. Migrant. Frying pan to fire. New horizons. Space and time. Here and now. This raft, unanchored. These sails, some wind. Boarding pass. This shrunken earth. Put your finger on it.

ON FACES

As noun: surface, aspect, front.
Facade. Put on your best.
"The moment I wake up,
Before I put on my make up,"
sings Aretha Franklin.
Mirror stage, reflection. Narcissus.
Social I.D. First impression.
Young and smooth, fresh;
wizened, shrunken, lined.
"On an empty face," writes Gorki,
"even a scar is an event."

At fiftieth reunion, I search strange faces
for recognition. Familiar features
slowly rise. Is it you, me?
Are you in there? Friendly?
Name to face, face to name.

As verb: confront. Affront.
Face to face. About-face!
Make a face, disgust or joy.
Two-faced. Baby Face Nelson.
See past and future, Janus-faced.

Funny: stretched mouth, red ball nose,
oval eyes. Expressive or un-.
Poker face. Deadpan. Bare-faced.
Can't keep a straight one? Actors need many.

My sculptor-nephew's series of
plaster masks, inspired by Ancient Greek
performers' masks and those of
Japanese Noh, have hung
on my sister's wall since his death.
My favorite wears mirrored sunglasses;
another, fingers knit, covers
its eyes like the first monkey;

a third yawns with hippo mouth
echoed in nostrils, eyes half-lidded.
A fourth has yellow, hollowed eyes,
mouth pursed and set, while cracks
spread across cheeks, nose, temples
and forehead, like earthquake rifts.

Face paint. War paint.
Faceless mob. Pale. Red.
Pandemic's PPE. Nothing to read but eyes.

On the face of things.
Effrontery. Emojis. Sketch artist.
Mug book. Yearbook. Facebook.
Face the music. Phantom of the Opera.
Stephen Crane's "The Monster":
"His face had…been burned away.…"

Half her jaw lost to cancer,
and after years of failed restorations,
Lucy Grealy learned to face up to her face.
Face down others. Keep face.

Perseus beheads Medusa with a blow
directed by reflection in his shield.
Then drops the head in a sack,
careful not to look or turn to stone.

Look me in the face. Say that again to my face.
Drones, or bombs from 30,000 feet.

The blind, or lovers in dark,
trace ours with their fingertips.

Lincoln closed his eyes, while being
greased with vaseline, then
bandaged with plaster-saturated gauze;
breathed through nostril holes
until the plaster set. At Huntington Museum,

accustomed to the photographs and paintings,
I'm startled by his life mask on display:
creases, warts, eyebrows, and all,
life-size, intimate, 3-D.
And then another, after death: older,
bearded, skin and mouth gone slack.

Fac-similes. Likenesses.

Children's fleeting as they grow.
The plaster sculpture of my wife's,
age six, an heirloom
on our family shelves through
child-raising and grand-parenting.
Her father, before his moving out,
had had her pose, his favorite of four;
sculpted from clay on armature;
then cast. I recognize her now,
heavy in my hands. Beloved.

Webster "saw the skull beneath the skin."

Here come the scary ones,
S.W.A.T.-teamers, robbers, klansmen, executioner.
Humanity obscured.

"Happy, happy, happy, happy face…"
"Though your face is charming, it's the wrong face…."
In masquerade, the familiar voice.

ON CHARACTER

Moral, psychological,
or literary. Round or flat.
Sound or flawed.
False or true.

Integrity. Mettle. Values that s/he
lives and stands for.
Wo/man for all seasons.
Fair weather friend.

Self-improvement.
Character building!
Ben Franklin's checklist
of virtues. Among the thirteen,
Industry, Chastity, Humility.
Then note to self: "Imitate Jesus and Socrates,"
which sent D.H. Lawrence howling.

(The psyche is impulsive
and instinctual, Lawrence believed,
not rational or mechanistic.)

S/he's a real character,
meaning oddball. Eccentric.
Laughable, admirable,
or obsessed.
Like twisted apples
with sweetness gathered
on one side.

Jonson's comedy of humours
supposed an imbalance
of secretions ("liquids")
from gall bladder, spleen, heart,
and brain. An overdose of one
determined personality type:
choleric (quick to anger),

melancholic (gloomy),
sanguine (optimistic),
phlegmatic (cool headed).

"Most women have
no characters at all,"
confides an 18th century lady
to Alexander Pope,
leading him to
condemn and admire:
"Tis to their changes half their
charms we owe…
power all their end, but
Beauty all the means…
woman's at best
a contradiction still."

Know thyself. To thine
own self be true.
Polonius (stuffed shirt
and hypocrite) to Laertes
or Lord Chesterfield to his son.

Enter Shrinks, Inc.,
Freud and Jung.
Therapy by talk or drug:
"I wot not by what power,
but by some power it is…
[I've]…come to my natural taste."

Egos pre-programmed by
religion, schools, commercials
or Hollywood.

Borges theorized
the creator of Falstaff and Cleopatra
—each a carnival of types
defying summation—

"had become instinctively adept
at pretending to be somebody,
so that no one would suspect
he was in fact nobody."

Self and idea-of-self.
How do I catch
my own imagination?
Who do I mean to be?
Who can I stand to be?

ON COMPENSATION

Com as in together,
pens as in pensive.
Management and labor
usually disagree when it comes
to skills, wages, and workloads
unless arbitration forces them
to *think together* and settle.

To make up for losses or inequities;
to reward labors well done.

Equal pay for equal work!
Merits recognized, *not* sex
(except for sex workers).

Docked pay, or bonus?

Government legislates
minimum wage, e.g. $15 (less tax);
employers must carry
worker's comp insurance
to cover work-related injuries.
Still, the undocumented and needy
accept less "off the books."

Earning and deserving.
You couldn't pay me
to do *that*! Low pay, or over-.
Interns and apprentices work
for trade skills and experience.

The self-made or fortunate
insist: no free rides. Work-fare.

And then there's volunteerism,
my something for nothing.
Pitching in for common good.

We compensate for weakness
(sometimes) with wisdom and wit;
for blindness with heightened
hearing, taste, smell, and touch.

The golfer or marksman
aims above and to the side
to compensate for gravity and wind.

One hand washes the other.

The gambler plays for risk
against the odds.
Sly hands against dealt.

Money works too, earning interest
for the lender; borrower pays.

Convicts pay their debt
with deprivation and cloister.

Save for seasons of need.
Gift to loved ones and causes.
Can't take it with you.

The self-reliant R.W. Emerson
believed that true rewards
are meted in the next life.

In this one, meanwhile:
"All infractions of love and equity…
are punished by fear," and
loss teaches "growth of character."

Pass it on.

ON PROPERTY

Philosophers and monks disavow it.
Things of this world:
Versailles, Yasnava Polyana,
Mar-a-Lago or King Tut's tomb.

Thoreau's twenty-eight-dollar-
and-twelve-cent cabin.

We stake out territories, as do birds
with song—my tree, my nest.
Even the homeless, my sleeping bag,
shopping cart, my steam grate.

Unaccomodated Lear:
"Off, you lendings...
Thou art the thing itself."

Tsunami, tornado, wildfires
artillery or rockets
leave consumer goods
among the ruins.

Your TV or mine, inner-spring mattress,
mass-produced dolls and bikes.
Just things, we say. Got out alive.

"Every man has a property
in his own person,"
asserts John Locke.

The proprietary lover warns
"remember when a dream appears,
you belong to me,"
though lovers aren't property.

Covet not thy neighbor's wife
(or husband), trophy or not.

Covet not the swimming pool
the new SUV, the greener grass.

My teenaged son
prized his rap CDs, his DVDs,
his posters, his laptop,
his boxer underwear,
his Red Sox caps, his basketball
shoes, his dress shirts and T shirts
and faded, pre-torn jeans:
"my Life," he called them.
Blamed us if we touched
without permission, or
mixed in family laundry.

I drove him to college
mattress tied to roof,
back seats crammed
with impedimentia.

God bless the child
that's got her own.

Neighbors expect us
to keep up our house,
bushes pruned, grass mowed,
fresh paint. No eyesores
or neglect.

Property taxes hire police,
for fear of vandals, thieves,
or home invaders.
Some of us keep guns.

"What is the effect of property
upon the character?"
E.M. Forster asks.
It makes him feel "heavy,"
he says. Too heavy

to pass through the eye
of a needle.

As a boy I envied
birds, dogs, and wildlife
the right to cross
suburban yards,
blind to human borders.

And what of
public lands, parks, and commons,
owned by town, state, nation?
"This land is our land
From California
to Manhattan island,"
sings Woody Guthrie.

European ancestors colonized,
homesteaded, and fought
indigenous peoples
as well as each other
for the continent.

"The land was ours before
we were the land's," wrote Frost.

Whose island was Prospero's?
Sycorax's? Caliban's? Arial's?
Was Prospero the colonist,
or philosopher king?

In More's Utopia, Hythloday
argues: "where possessions be private…
it is… almost impossible
that the weal-public may be
justly governed."
And More's retort: "Methinketh
that men shall never there live wealthily
where all things be common."

Is this my poem,
or ours?

PART TWO

DOCTOR

My brother the cancer surgeon refused
to "prolong his dying."
Smoking left more cancer than lung.

He had married his fiancé, Maureen,
bedside, just days before.
His three estranged sons appeared.
"Gold digger," they whispered.
"She turned him against us."

My wife and I had driven down,
Boston to Cherry Hill, NJ.
Maureen had called. And called
my sister in Pasadena,
my brother in Colorado.
They'd phoned goodbyes.
No use coming, Chuck had told them.
Before they got here
he'd be dead.

Bare chested, he lay
pillowed and cranked to sitting.
TV tuned to golf overhead
on the far wall. Second bed
stacked with photo albums
spread to memories
of their recent month in Kenya,
where he'd volunteered and done
three hundred operations.

After divorcing the boys' mother,
who'd been unfaithful,
he'd played the field for ten years;
then dated Maureen for ten.
"We're engaged," he'd announced,
"although we both know better
than to marry." They traveled

by Concorde to Paris,
vacationed in Cabo; they visited
us in Boston, Jack in Colorado.

Tired of phony malpractice suits,
he'd retired early. "You have a gift,"
I'd objected long-distance.
"You can't just walk away."
"Oh, yes I can. It isn't easy, but I can."

Without prior training,
Maureen had assisted him
in Kenya where they also played
as tourists, first class.
Golf clubs. Hot air balloon.
Safaris in the game preserve.

He had spoken to me about
his will. His sons only called
for money, he said.
Would I serve as his executor?
He wanted to leave half
for Maureen, half for his grandchildren,
in trust for their educations.
I'd finally asked if he was sick.
He was fine, he'd said.

He had one favor now, in private.
Back at home, get a copy
of his birth certificate;
Fedex it to Maureen
to make the paperwork easier.
We kissed. My eyes welled.
"I don't like knowing I'll never
see you again," I said.
"It was a good life," he told me.
"Love you, guy."

He summoned everyone.
Wrote out thirteen checks,
ten thousand each (the maximum

allowable for gifts).
Each check seemed
like part of him, this bread
for this body.

We drove back home.
Maureen kept us updated.
His sons hovered still.
Morphine doses were enough
to kill him. He hallucinated.
Asked to die in her condo.
But no, the hospital was fine.
He'd be better cared for,
easier on her. She wept.
Ready to take him, but also alone.
She wouldn't know what to do.

Heat wave. Power failure.
By candlelight, I drew a bath
but the drain wouldn't close.
As I lay naked, knees drawn up,
a steady trickle. Breath by breath,
Chuck's life ebbed.

I sat up, pushed myself out.
Maureen called. He was gone.

ON GHOSTS

Ghosts haunt guilty dreams,
Richard's and Brutus's,
though no one else can see
other than the audience. Horatio
speaks to the ghost on the battlement,
yet only Hamlet hears its news,
its call for revenge.
Then in the closet scene, the ghost
appears to be Hamlet's hallucination.
"Whereon do you look?"
his mother asks, and Hamlet:
"Do you see nothing there?"

Banquo's ghost unmans Macbeth,
prompting his outcry before guests:
"Shake not thy gory locks at me!"
And his Lady's hushed rebuke:
"You look but on a stool."
The audience of course, looks on
actors (the Lady, a boy),
props and stage. Director's choice
whether to show the ghost or not.

Shakespeare's ghosts suit all
the critics argue. A skeptic,
Catholic, or Protestant
would each leave the Globe
with her/his idea of ghosts confirmed.

We're spooked by needing
more to love than death.

Horatio asks the ghost
Why do you come back?
To pass on clues to buried
treasure? To forewarn?

In James Agee's
A Death in the Family (1957),
Jay's wife Mary is mourning
with family when they all sense
a presence, which she knows as his.
"Stay near us all you can…" she tells him;
"[The children are] all right, my sweetheart,
my husband. I'm going to be all right."
Hallucination the others think.
Thought transference.

Paranormal researchers call such visits
"crisis apparitions," theorizing
they might be telepathic signals
sent while dying; or perhaps
"produced unconsciously by mourners
to console themselves." Others
consider them "guardian angels
sent to comfort the grieving."
No one has hard proof.

Psychics, swamis, fortune tellers,
spiritualists and voodooists abound.

Virginia Woolf's Mrs. Ramsey
(modeled on her mother)
is still a unifying force
ten years after her death;
brings her scattered family
together to resume their expedition
to the lighthouse.
"If they shouted loud enough
Mrs. Ramsey would return,"
thinks Lily Briscoe, her friend.

Spooky! Spooked.
Cartoons make the afterlife
cute in Casper's case,
though the Friendly Ghost

died as a child. He interacts
with mortals. Floats around
and passes through walls.
He seeks playmates.

Ghost in the machine
(a closed-circuit TV
in the case of Almereyda's Hamlet).

For romance, we've got
Bruce Rubin's *Ghost* (1990),
invoking wishful lore such
as spirits learning to kick cans
and borrow living bodies.
Hence Whoopi Goldberg
volunteers to be Patrick Swayze's way
of kissing Demi Moore.

Ghost Busters (1984),
pits a team of parapsychologists
against malevolent ghosts.
Who you gonna call?

Stephen Speilberg's *Poltergeist* (1982)
goes for horror instead of laughs.
A greedy developer builds
tract houses over a cemetery,
stirring spirits to attack
one unwitting family;
reach through TV screens,
animate toys, and abduct
their youngest child.

Pale as a ghost.
You look as if you've seen a ghost.
Not a ghost of a chance.
If he knew, he'd turn
over in his grave.
Ghost writer! Client takes credit.

Halloween fun
with fake blood and make-up,
sheets for costumes
(recalling winding sheets)—
give or take the Egyptian Mummy
wrapped in Ace Bandages.

Decaying bodies. My neighbor's
yard decorations, tombstone with
hands reaching out of the ground

Philip Guston painted ghosts
as convivial klansmen,
hard-drinking, burger-chomping,
chain-smoking, free behind masks
to trade opinions about life.

The ghost of the past. The burden
of tradition. Great works, great lives
precede us. Shoulders to stand on.
My father's spirit is within me;
or my mother's, or both, still fighting.

Spirits of absent ones
live in my heart. And mine
in theirs, to comfort and inspire.

I did hear voices once, alone,
during a long run in the Sierras:
mother, father, brothers, nephew,
friends, all gone. Keep going,
each said. Do your best.

Young Hamlet
one mission accomplished
forever haunts Horatio
restless for words.

ON STATUES

A kids game: freeze!
If the kid who's it
sees motion, then you're it;
if she turns away, you move,
then freeze in different position
before she sees.

Were Medusa game
she'd turn everyone,
moving or not, to stone.

Stasis. Stationary. Static. Stature.
"A three dimensional representation
usually of a person, animal,
or mythical being
that is produced by sculpturing,
modeling or casting."

Frozen and larger than life.
Graven images.
Tribute to power, public importance,
character and deeds.

Yearning for permanence,
to be remembered, if not worshiped.

"My name is Ozymandias, King of Kings.
Look on my works, ye mighty, and despair!"

Props for anxious tyrants:
Lenin. Stalin. Il Duce. Chairman Mao.
Sadam's with chain and tackle
Toppled from its pedestal
in Firdos Square

The Colossus of Rhodes
(depicting Helios, the sun god)

was a seventh wonder
in the ancient world, but
collapsed in an earthquake.
"Pliny the Elder remarked
few people could wrap their arms around
the fallen thumb
and that each of its fingers
was larger than most statues."
Afraid they had offended Helios,
Rhodians "declined to rebuild it."

Statues portraying ideas
or mythical figures
are modeled for by
anonymous flesh:
Michaelangelo's David,
Venus De Milo.

In keeping with More's *Utopia*
thinkers in Boston's Public Garden
outnumber warriors. Besides
George Washington on his steed,
and a few others, we have
George Robert White (philanthropist),
Edward Everett Hale (author, historian, minister),
Wendall Phillips (orator and abolitionist),
Charles Sumner (Senator during Civil War),
and William Ellery Channing
(Unitarian preacher and theologian).
Their bodies, aged, draped
in robes or humble suits
seem beside the point.
All are male, of course.

Easter Island long ears.
Lincoln Memorial.
Statue of Liberty.
Mount Rushmore's presidents
(with Chief Crazy Horse in progress).

Meditating Bhudda.
Crucified Christ.
Virgin Mary.
Wooden Indian to sell cigars.
8000 terra-cotta soldiers to protect
Qin Shi Huang.

History is written by conquerers.
Pagan masterpieces were
subjected to iconoclasm,
noses and genitals chipped off,
crosses carved on foreheads.

What to do now with
with monuments of
Confederate racism?
Deface, destroy, or store them
out of sight?

Rodin's marble
brings flesh to mind. The Kiss.
The Thinker. Don't touch!
And yet...

What fine chisel
Could ever yet cut breath?

Oh, she's warm! gasps Leontes.

His wife on a pedestal:
Standing Woman, 1932,
by Gaston Lachaise
in the MoMA garden.
Statuesque!

Holographs.

I joke with my wife and kids
about final wishes.

Get me to the taxidermist.
Have me stuffed.
Keep me in the closet,
a mannikin or hat-rack
for children to mock.

Pass me down, an heirloom
as curious and embarrassing
as the big fanged
polar bear rug
with glass eyes and yellowing fur,
the hunting trophy of
a forgotten relative.

At his retirement party
the beloved cop
grinned from our paper
beside his melting likeness
sculpted in ice.

ON RANK

"Lilies that fester smell
far worse than weeds," the poet writes,
warning that aristocrats, .
who sink (like Falstaff) to self-indulgence,
villainy, and cowardice are more offensive
than peasants, who lack their
opportunities and breeding.

Macbeth agrees: "[if] you"re not
i' th' worst rank of manhood, say 't."
Likewise Dante with his hierarchy
of sins and sinners, and even William Empson:
"If W.H. has festered, that at least makes him
a lily, and at least, not a stone;
if he is not a lily, he is in
less danger of festering."

From Private to General,
military ranks confer authority and duty.
Festering is cause for being demoted,
stripped of rank, or cashiered.

Unions have their rank and file,
led by elected officers. When officers
clash with management, they order
members out on strike.

To rankle is to upset
and anger. A rank amateur is one
with less skill and experience than pros.
The ablest weaver, tinker, carpenter, or tailor,
is clueless about performing plays.
Dyer's sons are upstart crows.

Rank suggests, along with
relative standing, that breakers of rank
stink in their attempts.

While "smell is the mute sense,"
according to Diane Ackerman,
English seems weaker than
others for ranking rankness.
According to Popular Science,
"An Indigenous Malaysian Language
Describes Smells As Precisely
As English Describes Colors."*

Smells may reek, be pungent,
stale, sour, rancid, putrid, fulsome, rotten,
sulfurous, noxious, disgusting, nauseating,
suffocating, unbearable. Pee-yew!
We cover mouths and noses at the stench.
Gag, like garbagemen; or like cops
examining a corpse. Funeral flowers,
especially lilies, cover the corruption.

And then there's the titan arum,
aka "corpse flower," that rarely blooms and briefly,
smelling like rotten meat to attract
the flies that pollinate it.

*https://www.popsci.com/article/science/malaysian-language-describes-smells-precisely-english-describes-colors/.

ON CANDIDATES

Truth-tellers, whose *candor*
Means whiteness, or brilliance;
whose *candid* statements are
honest or frank.
From the Latin, *candere*
(to shine or glow)
and *candidus* (white).
Smile! You're on candid camera!
Unposed, unguarded.
Roman senators wore white
like brides in purity
or ghosts in winding sheets.
For every Coriolanus,
a Brutus, Antony or Caesar
honorable men.
He words me, girls.
Degraded symbols
for their times and ours.
(Hilary, even, in her power suit,
whose worldliness I voted for).
Performers and mass-medians.
Slogan slingers,
applauding for themselves and us.
Mr. and Ms. Deeds
go to Washington,
where sincerity is a social vice.
Promise-maker, obfuscator.
Even *candles* give light.
"She doth teach the torches
To burn bright."
Can't hold a candle to her.
"All the darkness in the world
Cannot extinguish the light
Of a single candle,"
according to St. Francis.
Anne Frank agreed.
And *candling*, of course
Exposes bad eggs.

ON AGENCY

Winged or fallen;
Gabriel? Moloch?
Rule in Hell or
Serve in Heaven?
Natural or supernatural?
G-man or foreign?
Secret or free?
Or maybe chemical.
Agent Orange.
From the Latin *agere*.
In the driver's seat.
To steer, brake, accelerate.
For women free will.
The heroine drives the plot,
active, not passive,
contrary to Hawthorne's
Georgiana, say,
or maybe not, since
"Hawthorne grants her at the end
a slight touch of
The satisfaction of revenge"
(quoth Judith Fetterley).
Exerting power.
Think of Grace Paley's
open destiny.
Tillie Olsen's "She is more than this dress
On the ironing board,
Helpless before the iron."
My possibility, my responsibility,
insists my 20-something niece,
echoing my 40-something daughter,
my 60-something wife.
My body, my self.
My destiny.
Unless we enlist
one who acts for,
in the interests of,

at directions by a client.
Literary agent, fiscal agent,
real estate agent, lawyer,
shop steward,
elected official.
Together we stand,
empower and resist.
Collective agents.
Agents for change.
All lived no less by powers
involuntary and strange:
That isn't/wasn't me!
"My eyes have seen
What my hand did."
"Keep your hands to
Yourself!"

ON DESPAIR

Most men lead lives
of quiet desperation,
proclaims Thoreau.
Hemingway's old waiter
prays to Our Nada
who art in Nada
in his late night cafe.

"De" means without, "spe" means hope.

Friar Laurence counsels Romeo:
"Happiness courts thee in her best array,
 But, like a misbehaved and sullen wench,
Thou puts up thy fortune and thy love,
Take heed, take heed, for such die miserable."
Then recommends his death trick to Juliet:
"I do spy a kind of hope,
Which craves as desperate an execution
As that is desperate which we would prevent."

Richard III warns himself:
"I shall despair. No one loves me."
Hamlet's quintessence. Gloucester's blindness:
"We are to the gods, as flies to wanton boys;
they kill us for their sport."

In Bunyan's Slough of Despond:
"the sinner is awakened about his lost condition,
there arises in his soul many fears and doubts,
and discouraging apprehensions."

"To be poor is to be desperate," says Leonard Gardner.
Brokers defenestrated
in the Great Depression.
The best lack all conviction.
Jonestown's kool aid.
Suicide, the Savage God.

The pride and power of negation;
or need for relief.

Pop therapist Rollo May suggested
(in *Will and Power*) that
we look on loneliness as
"the capacity to love,"
as strength rather than weakness

Is despair, I wonder, the
capacity to hope?
On fortune's wheel
the worst returns to laughter.

At 24, draft-dodging with
graduate school exemptions,
in an Iowa City attic room,
I stare in the mirror,
deliberating whether to stick
a pin in my eye. Why, my loved ones
would ask, would he do such a thing?

Desperate for a second child
at 43, I gave up finally on
fertility therapies.
We chose to adopt.

At 64, I despaired of my son's
finding work;
with his MA in Marketing
he needed our support
while Manhattan headhunters
found him unpaid internships.
Four more years of dependence
before he was hired
full-time, an UX designer.

In struggles of writing,
I recall "negative capability,

that is when man is capable
of being in uncertainties, mysteries, doubts,
without any irritable reaching
after fact and reason."

Monkey on her back,
the addict despairs
until the twelve steps
teach solidarity.

In recovery
my friend James Brown
finds his own clean, well-lighted place
helping others to keep clean.

ON ORDEALS

A test of character. A trial.
Will you break, endure?

The ancient rites:
to walk on coals, for instance.
Physical punishment, not
as punishment, per se, but
as a lie detector.

Once proven guilty,
still worse awaited—
maiming, exile, death—
yet most, I'd guess, confessed
in order to escape the trial.

Imagine Hotfoot,
a rogue with feet so
calloused and quick
he always danced free.

Or Job, divine initiate,
"blameless and upright."
His earthly goods taken,
ten children killed, his body
afflicted "with loathsome sores,"
counseled by friends in patience,
rebuked for justifying himself
rather than God, then finally crying out
only to be shouted down by the creator
of Behemoth and Leviathan,
who nonetheless delivers him,
fortunes restored with interest,
ten new children born (same wife),
and blesses Job with ripe old age.

Or Oedipus, ignorant of his own
crimes while seeking to purify Thebes.

Or martyrs to belief,
Saint Joan, Sir Thomas More.
Anonymous self-immolators
protesting unjust war.

Soul-making, Keats thought.
Soul-revealing, Plato.

Raising children. Laboring for hire.
The rituals of grading, obliged
to sort my students' thoughts
as my best teachers sorted mine.

Politeness and forced smiles.
The marathon or mountain climb,
because it's there. To prove I can.
Football practice in high school.
Stacking hay bales on a baler sled.

Over-reaching as a writer.
Career reversals and demotions.
Petty rivalries and tenure fights.
Courting readers never found.

Root canals; accidents and surgeries.
Alcohol and other addictions.
Loved ones lost to sentences of pain.
Traffic jams on necessary routes.
Death camps.

We make the gods more just.

I'd run through fire for love,
flame-resistant; or perhaps duly purged.

Cremation, since you ask.

PART THREE

ON VERSIONS

The act of turning; to turn.
Versatile, turning with ease.

One account among many.
Matthew, Mark, Luke, or John.
A variant, or adaptation.
Vulgate or Latin.

Very, as in true. Verifiable.
Verisimilitude. Like truth.
Verso, the other side.
Conversion, turn
from one faith to another.

Aversion. Turn away
in hatred, fear, disgust.

Diversion, a joke or relief
from heavy matters, such as
Macbeth's drunken porter;
or advertising a fake attack
to adversaries: D-day at Calais!

Reverse, turn back. Revert
to childhood or an earlier draft.

Inversion. Turn inside out,
a child punishes the parent
or verb before subject.

Obverse: the heads to tails,
front of a two-sided coin, flag,
paper money, seal, or book cover.

Perversion: to turn to "ill effect,"
from use to abuse, natural to un-,
normal to ab-, though

in a world of differences,
one person's wrong is another's
delight in definitions.

ON CONFLUENCE

Mingle, flow together, join
like Pittsburgh's Monongahela and Allegheny
creating the Ohio.

Affluence comes from income streams
or even tributes from debtors
as well as from rivers swelling
from tributaries.

I'm only fluent in English,
halting in French and German.
However English itself is influenced
by many languages, just as rivers
are by watersheds and mountain snows.

Effluence: something that flows out.
Effluvium, usually waste.

Everything is flowing
according to Heraclitus, "No man
steps in the same river twice."

Eterne in mutability.
Time stop photography speeds up
cycles of growth and decay.
Thus do we ripe and ripe, rot and rot.
The earth, that's nature's mother, is her tomb.

The meeting of waters. Ocean currents.
The Gulf Stream, a river flows in water.

Walden Pond is fed by deep, cold springs.

Yoked purpose. Human chains.
Marriage, friendship, partnership,
and parenting. Gene and spirit pools.
From many, one. Go with the flow.

"Fields of inquiry," goals, discoveries,
memories and heritages.
Your thought meets mine.

Our "minds transfigured so together,
More witnesseth than fancy's images
And grows to something of great constancy."

Or merge to echoes in a Marabar cave.

ON DESIGN

The chair of mind. Forms impossible
to manifest. Intention. Approximation.

Designing villains, ambitious for power.
Richard, Iago, Edgar;
Designing women, Lady Macbeth,
Cleopatra, Volumnia.
Hamlet's surrender:
Providence in the fall of a sparrow.

Architect's blueprints. Schematics.
To mold, sketch, weave, or shape.
The best laid schemes o' mice an' men.
God's spiders feeding on God's moths:
"a darkness to appall." Problem solving.
Inventing. Edison's lightbulb
(despite such side-effects as
light pollution, which researchers warn
upsets our "circadian rhythm,"
and disturbs ecosystems).

My brother Jack's pipe layer.
After years of excavating ditches
with separate machines for digging,
spreading gravel, laying pipe, then
back-filling, he constructed and patented
an all-in-one, which reduced costs
and saved time. He didn't plan on geo-politics
and a poor economy, however. An order from
Iran was cancelled. Machines he'd built
stood idle and unsold. As loans
came due, he went bankrupt and
had to sell the patent.

Having lived for others, my mother said,
she'd planned her life in thirds: first for family,
second for world, third for self. But third

had been drained by caring for her mother
as well as for my father in retirement.
She'd run out of time. Design flaws.

Boston's streets began as cowpaths.
as opposed to Pierre Charles L'Enfant's
layout of D.C. with avenues
radiating out from rectangles.
No logic or foresight to Boston
except perhaps for barn dreams.

"Contingencies are endless,"
thinks Tolstoy's Field Marshall Kutusov
in reviewing attack plans; then sleeps.

Chart a course. Navigate by
stars and principles. Syllabi. Curricula.
Five-year plans for progress.
Business plans for profits. Put a man
on the moon. Social engineering.
Baby and child care. A literary magazine,
dream-driven, for readers who should exist.

Lillian Hellman to HUAC:
"I cannot and will not cut my conscience
to fit this year's fashion."

Designer dresses, drugs, and jeans.
Sustainability. Durability. Built-in obsolescence.
Passing fancies. Novelty. Pandering
to manufactured appetites.

And then there's improv, starting from scratch.
Great for jazz. Less so for houses.

In Richard Yates's story, "Builders,"
house design is a metaphor
for story telling. "I'm not even sure
there are windows in this particular house.

Maybe the light is going to have to come in
as best it can, through whatever
chinks and cracks have been left
in the builder's faulty craftsmanship."

At an MIT Augmented Reality conference,
I tried on goggles to see hundreds of
economic indicators and indices
presented in 3D, like a galaxy of stars.
Visualizing databases this way allows
money managers to chart investments
like Mr. Chekov on Starship Enterprise.

Try AAA for planning trips.

Organic design: "follow nature's principles
to build forms more natural than
nature itself." Or as with gardens
and wild-life, tame, shape, and graft
for human pleasures and needs:
"nature is made better by no mean
But nature makes that mean…
The art itself is nature."

However we're designed,
we seek to improve the image.

ON WONDER

Virgil's worn phrase,
mirabile dictu,
"wonderful to relate."
From *mira*, wonder.

To ad*mire* is to be
awestruck, amazed,
as at a *mira*cle or perhaps
a *mir*age, a wonder that is
only illusion and vanishes
on approach. And *mir*ror too,
that glass of miracles and wonders,
reflections of our outsides,
not always fair or even fun;
or that chronicle history of tyrants,
A Mirror for Magistrates.
On news of Antony's death
"When such a spacious mirror's
set before him, he [Caesar]
must needs see himself."

The wonder too
of lost love found, as in
The Winter's Tale or *Pericles.*
"They looked as they had heard
of a world ransomed, or one destroyed."
"Such a deal of wonder is broken out….
that ballad-makers cannot be able to relate it."
"It is required / You do awake your faith."

The dead revived.
Stories of the inexplicable,
loaves and fishes, walk on water,
parting seas, war's end, happy days,
seven wonders, life itself:

"before our eyes, the miracle
went out of my mother,"
writes William Gibson,
author of *The Miracle Worker*.

As for admiration,
it's come to mean "a tepid regard."
And wonder names white bread.

ON GLAMOR

"Glamor" means magic,
derived from grammar (fr.);
since in the Middle Ages
scholars, i.e. grammarians,
were "viewed with awe"
by the vulgar (who couldn't
speak Latin); and learning
was associated with wizardry
and the occult.

That old black magic
that you do so well…

Perhaps what grammar
brings to language,
beauticians bring to looks.

Rules of usage and syntax,
correctness of style,
a rhetoric of charms.
Come hither stares. Eye-liner,
false lashes, lipstick, rouge,
hair style and dye, straightened
and white teeth, lean
fitness, smooth skin.
Try a makeover, you too
can be a sorceress. Or sorcerer
(though men are likelier
to seem handsome or charismatic
than glamorous).

Clearly grammar improved
Eliza Doolittle's social prospects.

Different religions extol
plainness; distrust
glamor's sensory appeal.

A girlfriend once
told me she took holidays to
Puerto Rico where men
loved her thick ankles
as symbols of prosperity.

At six months, supposedly,
babies recognize their
mirror image as "I,"
and are forever caught between
hating and loving this
"other." Narcissus
drowns in his image;
Snow White's Mom
becomes murderous.

Beware the beauty myth
warned Naomi Wolf in 1991,
which enslaves women and
and requires them to
captivate. In 1962,
even Betty Friedan
feared aging to look
like her mother. There is
no objective hierarchy
of beauty, Wolf proclaimed.
We can refuse the trap.
"The next phase of…
women together…depends
…on what we decide to see
when we look in the mirror."

A recovering male gazer,
I welcomed Wolf's call
for "beauty that is non-competitive,
non-hierarchical, and non-violent."
For forgetting "to elicit
admiration from strangers, and
[finding] we don't miss it";

for "[awaiting] our older faces with
anticipation"; for regarding our bodies
as precious; for admiring "radiance,
light coming out of the face and body,"
as opposed to the body spotlighted,
"dimming the self."

Only for Romeo
doth guileless Juliet
teach torches to burn bright.
To others she seems ordinary.

And yet.
Who can resist Cleopatra's show?
No more contrived and breathtaking
entrance than hers at Cydnus
to conquering Antony (as reported
by Plutarch and echoed by Enobarbus).
As goddess of attires, cosmetics,
stage props, and allure
her spectacle beggars description.
Fancy outworks Nature.
She makes defect perfection.
Makes hungry where most she satisfies.

Cross-dressed Rosalind
advises the shepherd's cruel mistress,
that she's not for all markets.
Cross-dressed Viola
detects vanity in Olivia's
mock inventory of charms.
Shakespeare's women (played
by boys) see through
other's courtship tyrannies,
if not their own.
Is a world less concerned with
looks a better place?

One refreshing characteristic

of Mike Leigh's films are
his "ordinary"-, imperfect-
looking actors.

And what about the naturally
favored? Should they apologize
for their appeal and strive
to look commonplace,
if not invisible?

My granddaughter's quinceanera,
then high school prom.
My son's new bride, Judy.
My wife too, as a bride, and now
as mother of the groom.
Wedding pix. Not glamorous,
but shining, looking our best,
all glammed up.

Looking good, I compliment.
Am not, my wife says, fishing.
Are too, I insist.
Can't take my eyes off of you.
You're my favorite work of art.

As for poetry, well,
long live vernacular.
The language of real people.
Forgo the makeup and jargon.
Look in thy heart and write.

ON LUST

I've outlived lust, or think I have.

Schongauer's "Temptation of St. Anthony":
stings and nettles, swarms, talons,
clubs, and tugs. Demons like mutant
bugs and reptiles: bat wings, spines, scales,
snouts, whiskers, fangs, trying to
drag the levitating aesthete
back to earth.

Odysseus lashed to his mast,
shipmates drawn to ruin.
Circe's bestiary.

Immanuel Roth, Professor,
transformed to crowing rooster
by Lola Lola, The Blue Angel.

Walt Whitman ached with amorous love.
It's different from desire,
though I'm unsure how.
Impersonal, if not involuntary.
All appetite, blind.
Itch builds, heat spreads.
Cravings, fever.
I'm not myself:
The more intense, less choosy.

Paired butterflies, they hurt me
A deadly sin, least of seven.
Jimmy Carter: "I've looked
on a lot of women with lust.
I've committed adultery
in my heart many times."
Bill Clinton's sophistry:
No intercourse, no adultery.
Frosted blue dresses.

In Anderson's Winesburg,
preacher Hartman peeps on teacher
Kate Swift's window
from his bell tower:
"Then upon the bed…a naked woman
threw herself. Lying face down
she wept and beat with her fists
upon the pillow. With a final outburst
of weeping she half arose,
and in the presence of the man
who had waited to look and think thoughts
the woman of sin began to pray."

Sublimate, masturbate or procreate.
Misogyny, pornography.
The beast with two backs.
Noses, ears, and lips.
Goats and monkeys!
Yond simpering dame.
Fry lechery, fry.
Incontinent varlets.

Sex as the new frontier.
Summer of Love,
Woodstock, hippy carnivals,
pill-safe, pill-high,
before STDs. Rites of Spring
break in Ft. Lauderdale.

Mardian, the eunuch:
"I can do nothing
But what indeed is honest to be done;
Yet I have fierce affections and think
What Venus did with Mars."

Not often, but often enough
in fifty years of marriage—
despite divides of yours, and mine;
of rival needs, of blaming

setbacks on each other—
we knew the most passionate
love-making of my life:
whole-souled. Healing.
Together and graced.
Our own truest gods.

The young affects are now
defunct. The heyday
in the blood is tame.

Yeats and Freud were among
the first to be rejuvenated
by tissue transplants
from monkey glands.
Now Viagra promises, along with
"marital aids," to stir the coals.

We try too hard. Mistake the prize.
The graphic sex scenes bore me
with their posturing stars,
younger than our children.

Suck face, my love. Come,
hold me and be held.
Your breath and heartbeat echo mine.

The pride and dazzle of remembering
the triumphs of one flesh.

ON LEVITY

The opposite of gravity,
a serious person, grave as graves,
but also weighty, as in heavy matters.
Gravid. Levity is buoyant.
From the French, "lever," to raise.
To make light of hardships;
or to levitate, defying gravity,
rising in air as if in water—
unless we're astronauts in free fall.
Any muscle that lifts
is a levitor. An elevator
lifts us from our day.
We raise or levy taxes to pay for
levies—earthworks to protect
us from rising waters.
As yeast leavens dough,
we ferment deeper thought
with humor or with
counting small pleasures.
Colors in a garden,
dewy spider web aglow,
toss and nod of breeze-
blown, full-leaved trees.
Tug of kite, strike of
fish. Voice echos.
A sentence well-made.

ON GERMANS

Not citizens of Germany,
haunted by fascism,
V-2 rocketry and Nordic perfection,
but seeds. As in "all germens spill at once
That make ingrateful man!"
Germs. Wash your hands to kill
bad ones. Wear gloves and masks.
But also plant the good ones.
The germ of an idea, which
proves germane to problems of the day.
And which can grow, spread, and flourish
into grand designs. Fertile seeds
that germinate, like social justice
in Zola's novel, *Germinal*.
New starts. Spring itself.

ON MODES

The modern *mode,* as in modish
or contemporary, also means "fashionable,"
where tastes change from year to year,
and looks are designed by modistes.

Pie-a-la-mode with its scoop of ice cream
may or may not be fashionable.

Model manners are exemplary,
though those of models may not be.

The artist's model holds his/her pose,
to suit the artist's vision and beholding.

My sister models designer dolls
in clay or porcelain, one of a kind,
and more "disturbing" than fashionable.
They are modeled after those
of her sculptor son before he died;
then costumed by her daughter.

Model airplanes, trains, or ships
are scaled-down imitations.

Work mode, play mode,
meaning mind-set, skills, and readiness.
Modus operandi. The method of working.
Public and private. War and peacetime.

The outmoded can be modified
into the modern or mod. To moderate
is both to control and reduce;
to avoid extremes and keep debates civil.
The modest show moderate self-esteem.
In climate, the weather stays mild.

Singers modulate volume, tone and pitch.
However, modems are needed to modulate
and demodulate signals between
computers and optical cable feeds.

Modules are independent sets, or units
to be combined into some larger structure.
such as a building, bridge, or poem.

Modal, not to be confused with model,
concerns form rather than substance; or
subjunctive, imperative, indicative,
conditional, interrogative moods in verb.

Lillian Hellman refused to cut her conscience
"to fit this year's fashions," e.g. McCarthyism.

Fashion alone won't make the person.
"I have that within which passeth show,"
warns Hamlet. "These but the trappings
and the suits of woe."

Lear insists on keeping his train of knights,
"O reason not the need!" only to discover
"the art of our necessities…
can make vile things precious."

Shepherdess Perdita, after a costume change,
wonders, "Sure this robe of mine
doth change my disposition."

And then there is cross-dressing.

Millennials now demand "sustainability,"
a fashion that can be worn for years
and is "eco-friendly and ethically sourced,"
as opposed to "fast fashion," where trends
change overnight and garments are overproduced.
New services even help women to buy and sell
from each other's closets, rather than buy new.

"I do mistake my person all this while!"

As for me, I'm in retirement mode.
My daily wardrobe is casual, give or take
running shoes and athletic gear.
For weddings, funerals, or readings;
a class reunion, visits to distant family,
or a writers' convention, my bests are
a corduroy jacket I've worn for decades,
dress shirts, ties (wide and narrow), and slacks—
all passed down from my bro-in-law.

In airport or city crowds, I'm invisible.

My academic robe, faded from
crimson to pink, is up on E-bay.

When sick or in need of repair, I sport
an ID bracelet, and the latest Johnny.

PART FOUR

ON TREES

Though some of us hug them
as thick-skinned, long-lived cousins,
as shade-and-shelter makers, CO_2 breathers,
wind-breakers; though we have hearings
for them when they become troublesome;

though we love their tossing and
wind-seethe, their birds in song;
their fruits, berries and nuts,
lumber, fuel, pulp, and sweetened sap;

though we harvest and welcome evergreens
in parlors for the holidays;
though we plant trees in orchards and nurseries;
though we love to climb, swing,
and build houses in them as children;
though we wonder at their upward
thrusts, contortions and twists;
though we're dazzled by their fall colors:
count and read their rings
(even play them as records);

though naturalists praise the model
of collectivism through tangled roots,
where enzymes warn an oak of a new parasite
attacking a nearby birch or maple and
even deeper, the continental root-mass
serves as a kind of vegetable internet;

though our ancestors once
dwelled in them for safety;

though we celebrate them on Arbor Day;
still...we have our fears and fantasies.

What if they can move,
like Birnam Wood to Dunsinane

or Tolkien's ents attacking Sauruman
for military-industrial deforestation?

What if they have souls?
What if when we pluck their fruit,
they cry out and rebuke us?
What if they are nymphs
fleeing harassment, like Daphne,
and magically transformed?

What if the bough breaks?
What if we can't get down?
What if roots give and trunks
topple, crushing us below
in cars, or in our beds?

The standard Nordic Noir film
opens with a fly-over shot of
solid treetops stretching for miles,
beneath which savagery and sin
are hidden. The heart's forest.
Dante's. Hawthorne's. Freud's.

Friendly wolves lie in wait.
Paths are crooked and misleading.
We're on our own, no rescue near.
"We're not out of the woods yet."

The growth of trees
mimics the evolution of species,
according to Charles Darwin,
with higher, newer branches
replacing those below. Forms
fungal, vegetable, and animal are
all related by "common descent."

So we, in families, begin with
common ancestors, connect to sibs,
cousins, aunts, uncles, generation

after generation, grands- and greats-
of kin until we find ourselves
and progeny; or branch's end.

And at the Bible's root
there's paradise and knowledge's tree
tempting first parents with mortality.

A God-blink later, someone weaves a rope,
appoints the hanging tree, adds bitter fruit.

LEAVES

1. TREE

Each fall we anticipate peak foliage,
drive north to take in blazing hills
before the change spreads south.
Towards Halloween, scattered browns,
reds, and yellows fill our yards and
we rake and blow them into waist-high piles.
Years ago, after kids had fun jumping,
residents burned their leaf-piles,
and tanged the air. Now we pile
armfuls into bio-degradable yard-bags,
and put them out for town collection.
Each tree sheds until it's bare. The last leaf drops.
Dormant and skeletal (give or take
squirrel nests), the limbs and branches
bend with snow and ice, sway in winds,
and sometimes snap. But then
the sun's arc rises, days lengthen,
ground thaws, first buds appear
on branches. We see the tint of green.
And then full leaves, and blossoms.
It's pollen season: spring welcome, allergens not.
Each tree fills out, a photosynthesis
factory. Thick canopies of shade. Birds
sing in the reaches. Squirrels chase.
Layer on layer, separate branch clusters
are enlivened; they dance and shimmer,
whisper and whoosh. Have voices.
Look up, see greens glow; look down, see
patches and shadows keep time on the ground.

2. FIG

I've never touched or worn one.
Don't give a fig (to be honest), or even a fig newton.

Wikipedia explains, "the vibrant green leaf
has three to five lobes and a prominent stem,"
and is the size of a fielder's glove.

According to Genesis 1:3, Adam and Eve
"sewed together fig leaves
and made aprons for themselves";
not for camouflage, style, or warmth,
but for shame, particularly of genitals.

They'd lost their blissful ignorance,
and realized that the obvious way
their bodies differed from their Creator's
was in their reproductive organs.

Or so it seems to me, whose fourth grade class
was told to draw the outline of a human body.
Puzzled by what our teacher expected,
I never finished mine; left its crotch blank.

Masaccio in his 1420's fresco, "The Expulsion,"
painted Adam and Eve, once free
and perfect as pagan gods, now driven out
by an archangel with sword. Adam hides
his face in both hands, penis exposed; while
Eve weeps and covers breasts with her right hand,
pudendum with left. Some time later,
a censor added fig leaves for both loins.
For Stephen Greenblatt, Masaccio's Eve evokes
 "the naked women in those infinitely
cruel photographs taken by the Nazis."

The fall of man. Exit, east of Eden.
Aware of good and evil, but not yet of loss,
not of frailty, mortality, pain in childbirth,
predator and prey, war, or seasons' cycles.
And not of dreams, either: of love, growth,
mercy or redemption.

3. BOOK

"Turning over a new leaf" has nothing to do
with aprons, unless to put shame behind us.
It means new chance or start.   New chapter.
Books have leaves with paper milled from trees.
We leaf through their pages. Covers are boards.
A folio (cousin of foliage) is a large sheet,
folded and cut into leaves. Illustrations are interleaved.
Leaflets are printed handouts, or young sprouts.
What wit first saw this likeness?
"These trees shall be my books,"
vowed Shakespeare's Orlando.
"And in their barks my thoughts I'll character."

4. CLOVER AND TEA

Some believe that leaves of clover,
and of tea also, affect their fortunes.

The four-leaf clover, rarer than the three-,
but not as rare as the five-, promises prosperity
to its finder, especially for the Irish.
Each leaf symbolizes faith, hope, love, and luck.
A fifth promises financial success.
Having searched patches for decades,
I've never found more than threes.
Perhaps it takes a four to find one.

Reading tea leaves (aka tasseography)
is predictive, not a charm. Along with palm
readers and other fortune tellers,
tea leaf readers keep parlors on city blocks.
Loose-leaf tea is steeped in a cup.
Once the sitter drinks it down, the reader
swills around the residue, then turns the cup
over on its saucer, leaving leaf-clumps
to interpret. A heart-shape near the rim

portends a lover soon; triangles in center,
a good fortune later. Other symbols promise
insights, warnings, and encouragements.
Will I get pregnant? Girl or boy?
Will my team win? When do I buy?

For me, I'll keep my bet on Providence.
As Hamlet says, "The readiness is all."

5. TABLE

Our formal dinner table, inherited
from my mother, normally seats six. But also
can be expanded to eight or ten, thanks to
two extra leaves. We release a lever
underneath and pull the ends apart,
slide in each leaf, then close and lock.
It's all mahogany veneer, with only six
matching chairs, so we add kitchen chairs.
Occasions for full leaves are rare
since our children left. Shortened, the table
collects household clutter; and our habit
is to eat, plates in laps, in front of our TV.
But when we gather for holiday visits,
we're packed as close as an overbooked flight.
I'm at the foot, and Connie the head
(having brought in turkey, roasts, or ham
and other hot dishes); our children on both sides,
along with their partners and children (Ruth's at nine
and sixteen; David's with booster at one).
Sometimes a guest. Sometimes, my ghosts:
my parents, sister, and brothers. My missing friends.
Connie's absent loved ones. We pass dishes;
eat, shout, laugh, make toasts. Our seasons turn.

ON PRIVACY

"With so many brothers and sisters, I'd never had many opportunities for privacy. I liked to go into my mother's closet and sit there in the dark for the sheer pleasure of smelling her, at the same time knowing how annoyed she would be if she knew I'd invaded her privacy. I became a snoop....What was it like to be someone else?" —Lucy Grealy, AUTOBIOGRAPHY OF A FACE

Robinson Crusoe needn't worry,
in the open on his island.
No need to hide privates
from primates, swinging in trees.

Goldilocks invades the home
of absent bears, gone for a stroll;
tries out beds, chairs, and porridge,
slumming in her way.
Of course, they did go out
and leave their door open.
Lesser animals know better
than to intrude on the stronger,
but white children expect
a glad welcome everywhere.

If not a home invader,
in Manhattan, Goldie might
spy on the apartments opposite,
like the invalid in Rear Window,
like each patron of movies,
whether with strangers in the dark
or alone with streaming TV.

Respect the privacy of others
we're told. Each to her own.
Keep eyes modest. Don't
eavesdrop, stalk, snoop, or peep.
Mind your own business. Live, let live.

Privacy's a right, we think,
unless famous, enslaved, imprisoned,
or a child. "Castle Doctrine" laws
allow owners to shoot first,
assuming trespassers to be
predators or thieves. Ask questions later.

Along with fear, shame leads to
fig-leaves and shyness;
privies and shower stalls.
Bathrooms, locks and keyholes,
bedroom walls and changing rooms.

Distrust your spouse? Check pockets, desk,
wallet/purse, computer files, bank statements,
credit cards, i-phone. Or hire a Private Eye.

And what of show-offs? Flashers?
The brazen or indifferent? Naturalists?
Protesters with bull horns?
Door-to-door salesmen and evangelists?

Having a party? Be sure to invite
the neighbors so they won't complain.

Don't hang out dirty linen.
Don't live in glass houses.
Please, please don't practice drums.

Celebrities and public figures
feed on publicity, but then can't escape.
Having captured our imaginations,
they waive the freedoms of obscurity.

Memoirs? Autobiographies? How did
St. Augustine overcome sin? Ben Franklin
rise from printer's apprentice to founding father?
What secrets, trials, and lessons to inspire?

And what of writers, otherwise unknown?
Wordsworth shares his vision's growth.
Joyce his portrait of a word-drunk youth.
Robert Lowell suffers obsessions,
break-ups and break-downs; prays
for "the grace of accuracy."
Frank Conroy masters mania.
Lucy Grealy, in owning her anomalous face,
wins and offers kin. Such writers,
writes Tobias Wolff, teach
"self-awareness without self-importance,
moral vigor without priggishness, and
the courage to hang it all on the line."

More cautious talents miss the point,
rely on "hooks," or representing
the under-represented, voicing groups.
We get reality TV. Teen-age selfies. Self-promotion.
Gut-spillers. Barstool tear-jerkers.
Self-absorbed, public mutterers.
I'm here. I'm here. I'm here, too. Me!
Open-mic poetry readings mimic AA.
Hello, I'm Abigail. I'm a poet.
Sometimes they overstay their turns,
imposing on our manners; as we impose on
theirs, when our turn comes.

"I won't tell everyone. But will tell you."
For eyes only. Confidential. Top Secret.

The secret of strength is in my hair.
The Wyf of Bath tells us Midas's wife
swore she'd never tell about
her husband's donkey ears, but then
ran down to the lake and whispered
to the water: "Don't tell anyone…
My husband has the ears of a donkey!"
She couldn't help herself.

No identity theft.

No hacking into personal computers,
emails, cell phones. No robocalls, please.
No soliciting, unless it's Halloween.
No phishing schemes. Of course we're
warned never to put anything
in email we wouldn't on a postcard.

While mainly concerned about Big Brother,
and how personal information is farmed,
still we post our fool's faces and opinions,
and speak loudly into cellphones,
as if the strangers around us can't hear,
or not caring if they do.
And who has nothing to protect or hide?

Can't hear myself think. No idea
what I was thinking. Have to get away
to think. Think what you like.
Thought is free; action, not.

Some thoughts are too private
to be conscious. Sub- or un-conscious.
Re- or suppressed. Somatic. Acted out instead.
Lady M. sleepwalks, washing hands.

No hiding from divine all-knowing,
some believe, let alone from ourselves.

But at Walden Pond, my wife and I
swim out from the crowded beach
to depths a quarter mile from shore.
(We're tethered to neon-colored swim buoys,
just in case.)   We shed our cares and stress.
Occasional distance-swimmers slog past,
be-goggled and intent. Voices recede. Individual
human forms recede to specks.   Time slows.
We float on our backs, engulfed by sky.
Water deafens all but hearts and breath.

ON DISTANCES

Psychological, ideological,
social, ironic, physical,
and aesthetic, e.g.
Wordsworth's "emotion
recollected in tranquility."

Elbow room. Boundaries.
Claustrophobia: the MRI's
chamber of clicks.
Shrunken globe, cheap flights.
Blue marble from space.
Why are you so distant?
Marvell's Platonism: "[Our loves] so truly parallel,
Though infinite, can never meet."
Robinson Jeffers' post-apocalyptic yearning for
"The dignity of room, the value of rareness."

Memories, like "far off mountains turned to clouds."

Punitive: stand in corner.
Keep your distance. Avoid.
Restraining order.
Isolation, solitary; quarantine.
Shelter in place. Cabin fever.
Neighbors, masked, cross streets.

Hoagy Carmichael / Ned Washington Jones's
"The Nearness of You."
George David Weiss / Jerry Bock / Larry Holofcener's
"Too Close For Comfort."

Letters and messengers arrive
too late. Friar John's
quarantined in Mantua.
We can't tell Pyramus
that Thisbe only lost her scarf
as she escaped the lion.

Telepathy, smart phones, texting,
video calls from different zones,
climates, or from space;
words, thoughts, art, artifacts
from earlier lives, traces,
imaginings & dreams,
what use if still intangible?
Out of touch, we say.
Or keep in touch.

Binoculars may bring us closer,
or seem to; wrong-ends farther.

Out of sight, out of mind.
Fading into distance.
.
Other places, other times.

For germ's sake,
don't touch your face.
Mask up, wash hands.

In less contagious times
closest others touched our faces,
both present and immediate;
yet even bare-faced no one but the owner
knew what thoughts and feelings lurked.

I read my face with fingertips,
blindly, or watch myself
perform in mirror or on screen.

We mug for our ten-month-old
granddaughter on Face-time.
She breaks into grins and squeals
in seeming recognition,
keeping close. Two months
have passed since our last
in-person visit (three hours

each way, depending on traffic)
for the weight of her in our arms.

She's walking, even dancing now.

LOST

Several times the size of our back yard,
bordered by stone walls in a clearing
of dense woods, the Metfern Cemetery
holds 296 graves, with numbered cinderblocks
indicating the order of deaths from
1947-79, and marked by P for Protestant
or C for Catholic. No names.

The remains came from nearby institutions,
Fernald State School for the Feeble-minded
("the nation's oldest institution
for people with developmental
disabilities") and Metropolitan State Hospital
("an asylum for people with
mental illness"), both now closed.
Advocates for the disabled
forced the state to release the names
of those buried, which in turn
prompted a history teacher
and his class at Waltham's Gann Academy
to research their biographies
and post them on a special website
(http://www.metferncemetery.org).

My wife Connie and I knew none on this
as we first entered the woods of
Beaver Brook North reservation.
We'd been exploring public
hiking trails, masks at ready,
since the pandemic had closed gyms
and crowded the Charles River path.
The forest and wetlands of several hundred acres
on the Belmont/Waltham border and
a short drive from our home
promised miles of isolated, shaded hiking.
An online map showed
meandering trails, like veins on the back

of a hand. Our path rose and dropped
underfoot, from drumlin ridges
to gullies. Thick ranks of trees with vines,
bushes, wild flowers, and weeds. No wildlife yet,
just birds and squirrels. Now and then humans
intruded, masks up (or not), avoided us.
Some with dogs. A mountain bike.

After a mile, we'd gotten lost.
We followed one path, wider than others,
saw a sign in the distance,
a wall. A cemetery had been featured
on the map, I recalled, and here it was.
We had our point of reference.

While Connie checked her GPS,
I puzzled over markers with numbers,
but didn't bother to read more of the sign
than "Metfern" with some dates.
Anxious to make our way, we confused
directions, chose a path beside a marsh,
emerged onto a street and sidewalk
that joined Trapelo Road.
We'd found civilization, at last,
but now must follow sidewalks a mile
to Trapelo's intersection with Mill Street,
then left on Mill for another mile—
past the entrance to McLean's—
to our parking lot at Lone Tree Hill.
We should call an Uber, I joked.

Across Trapelo, I recognized
the entrance to Fernald State School
and its rolling, grassy acres.
However, the Welcome Center,
the only building visible from the road,
stood surrounded now by dirt piles
and heavy equipment. Being enlarged,
or replaced, I supposed.

I'd volunteered there shortly before
we met 48 years ago, I told Connie.
I'd answered an ad in *The Boston Phoenix*:
"Bored with the Square?...Put your energy
to work with retarded children."

With a new PhD and no prospects,
I'd driven out for an interview.
The young woman in charge asked if
I knew any mentally disabled people.
No, I answered, but I'd read about them,
seen them on TV. There used to be one
in our town, mascot of my high school.
(I didn't mention that I planned
to introduce a Down's Syndrome child
into my first novel, so needed to research.)

She'd shown me around. I'd start
in Farrell Hall, a new, one-story complex
for ages 6-12, girls and boys.
We passed a man shuffling by in
shorts and Red Sox shirt, grizzled crewcut;
he grinned toothlessly and waved.
We passed more stray walkers,
with their awkward walks and baggy
clothes. Rundown playgrounds.
And then first women.
We passed a "Chapel of Holy Innocents."

At Farrell, I met the supervisor and staff.
The kids were *innocents*, some bored,
some watching TV, playing games
or coloring in the rec room; others
in a classroom gathered around a teacher
who played piano and led them
singing *Mary Had A Little Lamb*.

At first, beaming with good will,
I helped the older kids to

read stories, try conversations,
play ball games or red rover.
We went for walks, holding hands.
I remember their faces lighting up,
although some troublemakers acted out
and needed staff to calm them.

The campus had forty-two buildings,
housed 2700 residents and staff.
Different groups were separated by age, sex,
and severity of disabilities. They had
a hospital, a gym, bowling alley, an inside pool,
a farm, a vocational building, a laundry,
a kitchen, a bakery, and a power plant.

The school's mission was "to maximize
development… either in preparation
for return to the community or as the basis for
a happy and useful life within the institution."
Over time, however, the school had become
primarily a refuge for severe cases,
causing the superintendent to complain
that they must struggle to find
"pupils suitable for parole and work
on farm and essential services."
Residents' destinies were mapped
like circles of the Inferno. They shifted
from ward to ward, group to group,
conditions worsening as they aged.

I lasted for three visits. Returning
to the young, agile, careless crowds
of Harvard Square, I'd felt disoriented,
carrying memories of the wheelchair-bound,
encephalitic dwarf, say, who spoke gibberish
but gestured ruefully, and had intelligent eyes.

Finally, I stopped on the hill above Farrell,
intending to report; but couldn't force myself
forward, nor could I keep from leaving.

The child I imagined in my novel,
is saved from institutional life
by her widowed father and the woman
he courts. "She belongs with us,"
the woman insists. "There nothing else
for her otherwise. Not even a chance."

On return from our hike, I studied
the trails, as well as local history.
Fernald had closed in 2014 (and the Metropolitan
State Hospital in 1992). The City of Waltham
bought the lands. Clients had been
sent from Fernald back to relatives,
or to private, community-based settings,
and to special education programs .

Lawsuits and settlements preceded
the closing—along with rising costs, and
post-Holocaust rejections of eugenics.
Former residents complained
of sexual and physical abuse;
of "little education and less affection";
of superficial and mistaken diagnoses;
of overcrowding; of boys in the 1950s
being used for medical experiments
 (e.g. being fed radioactive cereal);
of sterilizations; of forced labor;
of "warehousing for convenience,"
of solitary confinement for
captured escapees. Their stories
were widely publicized with release of
Michael D'Antonio's 2004 book,
The State Boys' Rebellion, followed by
PBS and CBS-TV documentaries.

Of course, once aware, Connie and I found
our way back to MetFern's graves.
I noticed that stone cairns had been balanced
on different markers by strangers

or by families, such as on C-125,
which the website identifies as
Adeline Ward, born in Lynn, MA, 1907,
lived with parents and three sisters until
committed to Fernald, 1951, died
of a cerebral hemorrhage,1968.
Most had markers overgrown: C-136,
Claude Moran, worked on the farm,
suffered burns in a shower,
then died a week later, aged 66.
P-124, Sally Kenorian, born 1959,
placed at 18 months due to her
Down Syndrome, died of pneumonia, 1962.
Row after row. Since 1979, Fernald's residents
had been considered residents of Waltham
and buried in the city's cemetery.

According to Gann's history teacher,
Alex Green, the Metfern dead
"were the least fortunate among
the thousands of inmates who
passed through these places."

One path leads to another.
Eventually we find home.

DeWitt Henry was the founding editor of *Ploughshares*. His books include *The Marriage of Anna Maye Potts* (winner of the Peter Taylor Prize for the Novel) and a trilogy in memoir concluding with *Endings & Beginnings: Family Essays* (MadHat), which was longlisted for the PEN/Diamonstein-Spielvogel Award for the Art of the Essay, 2022; and a collection of notes and essays, *Sweet Marjoram* (MadHat 2018). He has also edited several anthologies, including *Fathering Daughters* and *Sorrow's Company* (both from Beacon Press). His collection, *Foundlings: Found Poems From Prose* appeared in 2022. He is Professor Emeritus at Emerson College and serves as a contributing editor to both *Woven Tale Press* and *Solstice* magazines. More details are at www.dewitthenry.com

www.ingramcontent.com/pod-product-compliance
Lightning Source LLC
Chambersburg PA
CBHW030223170426
43194CB00007BA/846